Go West, Ox!

GW00888690

Written by Jeanne Willis
Illustrated by Woody Fox

Ox sat in a pen.

A pen is no fun.
Let me be.

Ox had a plan.

I can go west!
Not me.

I will pack a bag!
Slam!

Ox jumps into a van.

I can be on a jet at six!

Sat Nav!
But Ox hits a box.
Biff!

The van hisses and stops.
No! It is the cops!

Jump to it lads. Get the ox in the back.

Not me! The Sat Nav!